AEI LEGISLATIVE ANALYSES
Balanced analyses of current proposals before the Congress, prepared with the help of specialists in law, economics, and government

Issues in 1985 Agricultural Legislation

1985

99th Congress
1st Session

AMERICAN ENTERPRISE INSTITUTE
FOR PUBLIC POLICY RESEARCH
Washington, D.C.

ISBN 0-8447-0269-2
Legislative Analysis No. 54, 99th Congress
August 1985

Contents

1

INTRODUCTION

The perception of economic crisis in U.S. farming and the importance of current agricultural policies in curing it have heightened interest in the 1985 farm legislation and increased the likelihood of changes in U.S. farm commodity programs. Yet agreement on what changes to make, particularly on the maintenance of income protection for farmers through target price guarantees, had proved impossible to finalize in the Agriculture Committee of either the Senate or the House by the August recess. Many issues are as much on the table as they were when deliberations began early in 1985.

In the many bills that have been introduced, a few basic issues recur—how to expand U.S. agricultural exports, what to do with market support ("loan rate") prices, how large to make direct payments to farmers, what role production controls should play, and what to do about the financial squeeze in which many farmers find themselves. Each of these issues arises because of the existence of an economic problem of U.S. agriculture, respectively, a $10 billion decline in annual farm exports in the 1980s, accumulating government stocks of grains and dairy products, a $12 billion annual budgetary cost of the current programs, excess supplies of many commodities, and the "credit crisis" of 1984–1985. The substance of the 1985 act will be determined by the political resolution of these issues. This legislative analysis reviews the main proposals addressed to each issue and assesses their pros and cons.

2
BACKGROUND

New agricultural legislation is necessary in 1985 because the Agriculture and Food Act of 1981, which governs the main current programs, expires with the 1985 crop. The current programs operate through three main policy instruments:

1. The "target" price establishes a basis from which "deficiency" payments are made to farmers. For eligible production, the farmer receives a payment equal to the difference between the target price and a national average price received by farmers (or the market support price if it is higher than the national average price). These payments are primarily responsible for an annual cost of about $10 billion under the 1981 act.

2. The market support price, or loan rate, is the amount per unit that a farmer can receive as a loan from the Commodity Credit Corporation (CCC). The loan can be repaid in full (including interest) by forfeiting the commodity to the CCC. Thus the CCC will acquire grain whenever market forces push the market-clearing price below the loan rate, to the point that the observed market price is supported at or near the loan level (since farmers will not sell on the market for less than they can get from the CCC). This mechanism is responsible for the large CCC stocks that have plagued the programs from time to time.

3. Acreage reduction programs, or "set-asides," or "voluntary diversion" programs, all involve inducements to farmers to idle some of their cropland. The 1985 wheat program, for example, requires 20 percent of wheat acreage to be idled for farmers to qualify for deficiency payments or CCC loans and pays farmers $2.70 per bushel for wheat that would otherwise have been grown on an additional 10 percent of idled wheat land. The granddaddy of this program type was the 1983 payment-in-kind (PIK) program, the largest acreage reduction program in U.S. history; it was paid diversion with the twist that, instead of cash, farmers received title to CCC-owned commodities.

The programs for wheat, rice, corn, grain sorghum, barley, and cotton employ all these policy instruments. The programs for milk, peanuts, tobacco, sugar, and wool use similar instruments but with differing emphasis. The wool program makes payments to producers with no market price support or production control. Milk relies primarily on a market support price, with no payments. The peanut and tobacco programs are basically production control programs, and the sugar program works through restrictions of imports.

The 1985 legislation can change practically all the provisions of these programs. Whether it will do so depends on the legislators' economic and political judgments about the consequences of such changes.

3
Legislation Proposed

In table 1 are listed thirty-five bills on agricultural commodities introduced since the first session of the Ninety-ninth Congress during January–June 1985. It is not an exhaustive list. Moreover, many of the bills are ephemeral. The administration's proposal (S. 501/H.R. 1420), when its details were unveiled in January, was characterized as "dead on arrival" on Capitol Hill.[1] Many of the other bills do not stand a chance of enactment either. The administration's general approach—cut loan rates to stimulate exports, cut target prices to reduce budgetary costs, and eliminate acreage controls as unnecessary; in short, deregulate the commodity markets—is incorporated in many of the bills, at least in certain respects. Instead of dealing with each of these bills, we will examine the key issues, listed earlier, that are addressed in the various bills.

TABLE 1

1985 Farm Bills, 99th Congress

Designation	*Sponsor*	*Coverage*[a]
S. 250	Sen. Larry Pressler (R-S.Dak.)	Omnibus
S. 501	Administration's bill — Sen. Jesse A. Helms (R-N.C.)	Omnibus
S. 523	Sen. William L. Armstrong (R-Colo.) et al.	Payments to farmers of fragile lands
S. 598	Sen. Robert W. Kasten, Jr. (R-Wis.)	Payments to farmers of fragile lands
S. 616	Sen. Helms	Omnibus
H.R. 1629	Rep. Charles Rose (D-N.C.) et al.	Dairy imports

TABLE 1 (continued)

Designation	*Sponsor*	*Coverage*[a]
H.R. 1656	Rep. Dan Glickman (D-Kans.)	Omnibus
H.R. 1912	Rep. Charles W. Stenholm (D-Tex.) et al.	Production controls
S. 843	Sen. Thad Cochran (R-Miss.)	Omnibus
S. 884	Sen. Daniel K. Inouye (D-Hawaii)	Sugar
H.R. 2017	Rep. Rose	Omnibus
S. 908	Farm Bureau bill — Sen. Mitch McConnell (R-Ky.)	Omnibus
H.R. 2077	Rep. Glenn English (D-Okla.)	Omnibus
H.R. 2100	Rep. E. (Kiki) de la Garza (D-Tex.)	Omnibus
H.R. 2104	Rep. Ike Skelton (D-Mo.)	Export promotion
H.R. 2108	Rep. Ed Jones (D-Tenn.) et al.	Payments linked to soil conservation
H.R. 2112	Rep. Hal Daub (R-Nebr.)	Omnibus
H.R. 2128	Reps. Pat Roberts (R-Kans.) and Beau Boulter (R-Tex.)	Wheat
H.R. 2140	Rep. Wes W. Watkins (D-Okla.)	Export promotion
S. 1036	Sen. Howell Heflin (D-Ala.)	Omnibus
S. 1041	Sens. Rudy Boschwitz (R-Minn.) and David L. Boren (D-Okla.)	Omnibus
S. 1049	Sen. Pete Wilson (R-Calif.)	Export promotion
H.R. 2318	Rep. John Conyers, Jr. (D-Mich.)	Omnibus
H.R. 2330	Rep. Byron L. Dorgan (D-N.Dak.)	Omnibus
S. 1051	Sen. Edward Zorinsky (D-Nebr.) et al.	Omnibus
S. 1069	Sen. Patrick Leahy (D-Vt.)	Dairy
S. 1083	Sen. Tom Harkin (D-Iowa) et al.	Omnibus

TABLE 1 (continued)

Designation	*Sponsor*	*Coverage*[a]
H.R. 2464	Rep. Charles Pashayan, Jr. (R-Calif.)	Dairy
H.R. 2536	Reps. Jerry Huckaby (D-La.) and Arlan Stangeland (R-Minn.)	Omnibus
H.R. 2581	Reps. Terry L. Bruce (D-Ill.) and Glickman	Grain reserves
H.R. 2595	Rep. Jim Leach (R-Iowa)	Omnibus
H.R. 2600	Rep. Rose et al.	Tobacco
H.R. 2616	Rep. Barney Frank (D-Mass.)	Dairy
S. 1222	Sens. Bill Bradley (D-N.J.) and Slade Gorton (R-Wash.)	Sugar
H.R. 2715	Rep. Thomas A. Daschle (D-S.Dak.)	Omnibus

NOTE: Listed in order of introduction, between January 1, 1985, and May 31, 1985. Bills addressed to particular topics other than commodity programs—soil conservation, credit relief, food stamps, freight rates on government-sponsored exports ("cargo preference")—are excluded from this list. In some cases identical bills were introduced in both houses, but only one designation is given here.

a. "Omnibus" means that two or more commodities and two or more policy instruments are covered.

4
Issues and Arguments

Export Promotion

Governmental steps to boost exports, especially of grains, are seen as such an important issue that the Senate Agriculture Committee reported a separate piece of legislation on the subject (S. 1040), the Emergency Agricultural Marketing and Sales Act of 1985, in May, before either house had made any significant progress on the omnibus commodity program legislation. The bill authorizes the use of Commodity Credit Corporation stocks to pay export subsidies in kind and the commitment of $2 billion over four years to guarantee the repayment of intermediate export credit. It leaves much discretion to the secretary of agriculture on how to administer the program. The bill has not been enacted, but in May the Department of Agriculture announced its own $2 billion "export PIK" program of subsidies in kind of CCC stocks to exporters who sell at discounted prices in certain targeted markets. Through July 1985, however, no transactions had been consummated.

The export subsidy receiving most attention in the omnibus bills is the "green dollar" plan in S. 1041 (Boschwitz-Boren) and "export PIK" provisions in S. 843 (Cochran), H.R. 2100 (de la Garza), H.R. 1912 (Stenholm), and S. 616 (Helms). It is essentially a formalization of the use of CCC stocks to subsidize exports. Under S. 1041 exporters would bid for foreign sales at less than the going world prices, and the Department of Agriculture would then draw on CCC stocks to compensate exporters for the difference between market prices paid by the exporter in the United States and the discounted bid price received from importers abroad. Suppose, for example, that an exporter sold 10,000 tons of grain abroad for $90 per ton but had to pay $100 per ton in the United States to acquire the grain. The Department of Agriculture would give 1,000 tons of CCC grain to the exporter, who then would pay $900,000 for 9,000 tons in the U.S. market and receive $900,000 for 10,000 tons sold abroad (net of the exporter's margin for handling, shipping, and so forth). Many details must be worked out concerning who would be eligible to bid for this "export PIK" grain, how and when the bidding would take place, and the pricing of the foreign sales and U.S. purchases. But the essential economics are as described in the example.

Analysis. Disagreement is rife about the consequences of such a program. Some argue for it as a good way to target subsidized exports at markets recently captured by the European Economic Community (EEC) through its export subsidies. This was clearly Secretary of Agriculture John R. Block's approach in authorizing bidding for the first subsidized sales to Algeria and Egypt in June and July 1985. Some opponents have claimed that such a program would merely drive down world prices without expanding exports and therefore without strengthening U.S. markets appreciably. Others have argued that a small, targeted program will have no effects and a general, large export subsidy program is necessary.[2]

To assess the export PIK or green dollar approach, we need first to be clear about the standard supply-demand analysis of an export subsidy. In partial equilibrium terms (that is, neglecting effects on participating countries' balance of payments and hence on exchange rates of currencies), the effects are as follows. A generally available subsidy (that is, on all grain exported from the United States) worth, say, \$10 per ton of grain exported means that exporters will buy grain in the United States and sell it abroad as long as the margin between the U.S. and world selling prices is \$10 or less below the preprogram competitive margin. If exporters had been buying at \$100 per ton (New Orleans basis) and selling at \$105 per ton before the program, after its introduction they would make a \$10 per ton profit at these prices and would be willing to accept a spread of as little as \$100 (New Orleans) to \$95 (abroad), or \$102–97, or \$105–100, or \$108–103. Competition among exporters would result in some such combination, reestablishing the preprogram rate of profit in the grain exporting business, assuming the program had effective competitive bidding features so that exporters could not increase their profits from it.

The key result is that the U.S. price would rise and the foreign price would fall as exports rose in response to the subsidy. How much the U.S. price rose would depend on how much an addition to U.S. export volume influenced the internal U.S. market as compared with the world market. Since the world market is bigger than the U.S. market, we would expect a bigger price effect in the U.S. market, for example, the rise from \$100 to \$108 at New Orleans and the fall from \$105 to \$103 in the world market. But at some times and for some commodities the relevant world market can be quite small (or "thin"), so that the foreign price effect might actually be larger. All we can be sure of for a general export subsidy with competing exporters is that the U.S. price would rise, the foreign price would fall, and the spread between the U.S. and the foreign price would increase by \$10. (The main change in this analysis for noncompetitive exporters would be that the spread would not increase by \$10, because some of the subsidy would be captured by exporters as profit. But the U.S. price would still rise, and the foreign price would fall.)

FIGURE 1
EFFECTS OF 10 PERCENT EXPORT SUBSIDY

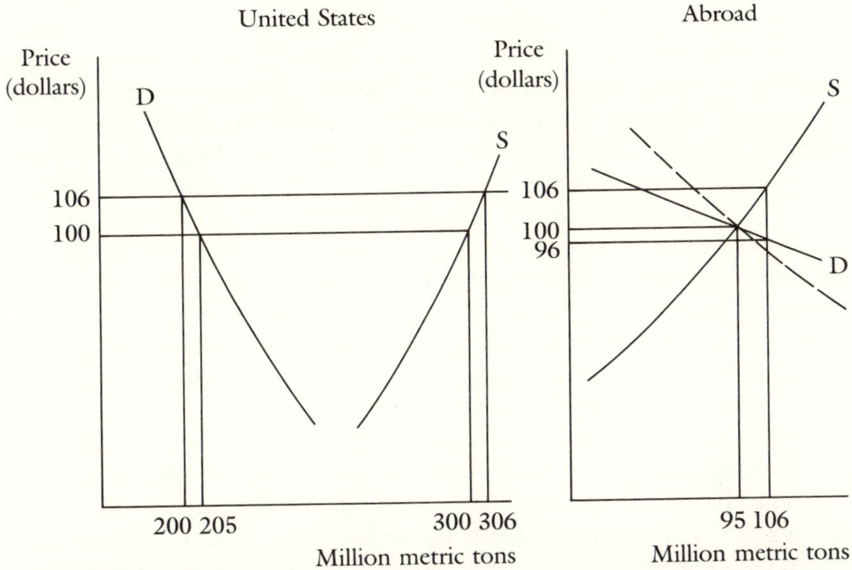

An example is shown in figure 1. For simplicity, it omits the exporters' margins, so that with no subsidy the market price would be $100 both in the United States and abroad. The export subsidy creates a $10 difference between the U.S. and foreign prices, the U.S. price being relevant to the supply of exports and the foreign price determining export demand. The quantities demanded and supplied both increase, the new market situation being shown in figure 1 as 106 million metric tons exported instead of 95 million tons with no subsidy. The export supply curve is derived as excess supply, that is, supply less demand ($S-D$), at each price in the United States. Its slope depends on the slopes of the U.S. *S* and *D* curves. As sketched, with figures roughly corresponding to U.S. wheat and coarse grains as an aggregate, the 10 percent export subsidy raises the U.S. price 6 percent and reduces the world price by 4 percent. In the United States this results in an increase in grain output of 2 percent (elasticity of supply of $^1/_3$) and a reduction of U.S. grain consumption of $2^1/_2$ percent (elasticity of demand of -0.4). Foreign demand for U.S. grain rises by 11 percent (elasticity of demand for U.S. exports of -2.8). These quantities depend on the elasticities assumed. All the elasticities are difficult to estimate, particularly the export demand elasticity. Some analysts would probably guess it to be closer to zero than -2.8. If it were half of -2.8, that is, -1.4, the export demand curve would be the dotted curve *D*. The 10 percent (dotted) subsidy line in this case results in a larger fall in the foreign price, a smaller increase in exports, and hence a smaller rise in the U.S. price than with the -2.8 elasticity.

The proposed new programs are not quite the same as a general support subsidy. Two important differences are (1) that the subsidy would apply only to some exports, not all, and (2) that CCC stocks would be used to pay the subsidy rather than cash. To analyze the consequences of these differences, refer again to figure 1. If the subsidy were paid on only a fraction of exports, say 20 million tons, this grain would be contracted in preference to unsubsidized grain, but since all market participants would know that U.S. exports would exceed 20 million tons, the scarcity value of grain would be determined at the margin by unsubsidized sales. (Compare: A family that drinks five gallons of milk per week is given coupons entitling it to a discount of 10 percent on the first two gallons it buys this week. How much milk will the family now drink this week? The reasoning here says five—there is no increase in demand.) Therefore, the market price both in the United States and abroad would remain at $100. Who would benefit from the subsidy scheme? This would depend on to whom the rights to deal in subsidized grain were awarded. Suppose that, as under the current program, the subsidy were targeted to a certain country, say Algeria. Algerian buyers would capture the benefits because U.S. exporters would have to bid competitively for the Algerian sales. If the rights to sell subsidized grain were allocated to U.S. exporting firms, say, 2 million tons to each exporter, then each could sell its allocation at the $100 world price and pocket the subsidy. Note that in neither case would there be any expansion of export demand, and consequently there would be no benefit to U.S. farmers. Why, then, use this kind of program?

First, one way to create some net addition to demand would be to offer a subsidy to Algeria to buy 2.5 million tons, say, when their purchases would otherwise have been 2.0 million tons. If they took this bait, there would probably be a net addition to demand (just as the five-gallons-of-milk family might increase consumption if offered a 10 percent discount if it would buy six gallons). Two situations could nonetheless defeat this addition: (1) the Algerians might offset the extra 0.5 million tons from the United States by purchasing 0.5 million tons less from the EEC, which the EEC would then sell elsewhere; or (2) the Algerians themselves might sell the 0.5 million tons at the world price and take a profit on the subsidy. In either of these cases the program would be defeated, and we would get the intramarginal result of no significant effect on market prices either in the United States or abroad.

In analyzing international prices, it is important to distinguish two concepts of price for traded goods. The first is the price plotted at the intersection of supply and demand—the market price at a port location for a certain time period—which indicates the marginal value of grain in trade.

The second is the "unit import value" or "unit export value," the amount a country pays or receives for traded goods divided by the quantity imported or exported. If a country's imports are all transacted for at the same market price, the two concepts of price give the same number. But if the United States provided part of Algeria's imported grain at a subsidized low price, then Algeria's unit import value of grain would fall even if the market price of Algeria's (marginal) imports remained the same. World market prices would generally be unaffected.

The bottom line is that an export subsidy can influence market prices only if it results in increased consumption by someone. Otherwise, no more grain is taken off the world market as a whole, with or without the subsidy, and no enlarged export outlet is created for any exporting country.

A second reason for a targeted approach exists even if there would be no overall U.S. demand expansion or price effect. The subsidy, if paid on sales to a market in which EEC exports are already subsidized, could be used as a weapon to disrupt and perhaps increase the cost of the EEC export subsidy program. The hope would be to encourage the EEC to scale back its general export subsidy program, and this would increase the demand for U.S. exports.

This reasoning suggests the economic sense that can be given to Secretary Block's statement that even though the targeted export subsidies are bad economic policy, we are going ahead with them.[3] It should be noted, however, that the EEC could work in the other direction—it could retaliate with a *larger* rate of export subsidy. If the EEC maintained its pre-export-PIK subsidies, it would lose exports, and its export subsidy costs would fall. So the EEC could readily increase its subsidy rate and recapture some lost sales. This would reduce U.S. gains from the export PIK program.

The scenarios outlined for targeted subsidies suggest that they could, by reducing prices in particular countries, increase U.S. export sales or that they could fail to reduce prices and leave U.S. sales unchanged. There is no way yet, however, to obtain the result predicted by some that the program could both fail to increase sales and reduce world prices. To obtain this outcome, we need to consider the second key feature of the proposed program, the use of CCC stocks instead of cash to pay the subsidy in kind. Those stocks would not normally be placed on the market until the price received by farmers reached about 1.7 times the loan rate for wheat ($5.60 per bushel) or 1.53 times the loan rate for corn ($3.63 per bushel). Prices this high are so unlikely that CCC grain is probably not considered part of market supply by grain traders. This means that using CCC grain for in-kind subsidies would increase the market supply available and therefore drive down market prices. Once price was driven down to the loan rate, however, the CCC would have to reacquire sufficient grain to maintain the market price at the loan rate, so that paying in kind would cause some useless recycling of grain out of CCC bins and back in again.

Why use the in-kind subsidy? Despite the preceding problem, it would reduce CCC stocks to some extent, and those stocks are costing the government more to store than the expected returns. Therefore, there would probably be an efficiency gain from reducing CCC stocks. Politically more important is the fact that the in-kind subsidy would not require an explicit budget appropriation, as a cash subsidy would. A replenishment of CCC finances might require a subsequent appropriation, but current budgetary pressures would be avoided.

Summary. To sum up the pros and cons of a targeted, in-kind export subsidy, as compared with a general export subsidy, the pros are as follows:

1. Budgetary savings would arise because the subsidy would not be paid on all exports and some uneconomic CCC stocks would be disposed of.
2. There might be an expansion of demand for U.S. commodities and a consequent rise in U.S. farm prices.
3. Disruption of EEC export subsidies might be a tool in negotiations on reducing trade barriers because it would make those subsidies more costly.

The cons are as follows:

1. Targeting might cause no significant addition to U.S. export demand, while release of CCC stocks could drive down world price.
2. If the price were reduced to the loan rate, stocks would recycle back to CCC.
3. If the program became too large, reduction in CCC stocks would provide less price stabilization in event of future shortages.
4. If the program raised U.S. farm prices, U.S. purchasers of livestock feed and grain products would pay more while foreigners paid less.
5. Disruption of export subsidies by EEC might lead to its increasing subsidies to recapture markets and dissipate U.S. gains from its subsidies.

Item 4 is a point of controversy not only for the targeted, in-kind export subsidy but for the general export subsidy as well. In figure 1, the gains to producers are $6 per ton on 303 million tons, or $1.82 billion. The cost to grain buyers is $6 per ton on 202.5 million tons, or $1.22 billion. So far that is a net gain for the United States, but we must also include the budgetary cost of the subsidy, which is $10 per ton on 106 million tons, or $1.06 billion. Adding these up leaves a net loss of $460 million. The loss is principally accounted for by the fact that $4 of every $10 spent on the export subsidy goes to foreign grain consumers.

These calculations depend on the supply and demand elasticities used, which are of course questionable. But no matter what elasticities are used, an export subsidy would still mean a net loss to the United States. Making the modification that might be most necessary, namely, considering a less elastic demand for U.S. grain, would increase the net loss to the United States since U.S. producers would gain less and foreign consumers would gain more. This is an irreducible disadvantage of any export subsidy. Paying $1.8 billion directly to U.S. grain producers would be more efficient because the $2.4 billion in export subsidies and higher U.S. consumer costs would not then be incurred.

Loan Rates

Most of the omnibus bills, with the notable exceptions of S. 1083 (Harkin), H.R. 2318 (Conyers), and S. 1051 (Zorinsky), lower loan rates for the grains, probably reflecting the widespread view that U.S. exports are being hindered by current loan rates and that CCC stocks are functioning to place a floor under world market prices and thus encourage output expansion by competing exporters. Current law sets the loan rates for grains at a level chosen by Congress, and the secretary of agriculture has limited discretion to adjust them when he finds stocks excessive. Two kinds of change have been proposed. The first makes the loan rate a fraction of a moving average of past market prices (S. 501, S. 616, S. 908, and H.R. 2112). The second makes the CCC loan repayable at the lower of the original loan rate or the market price at the time the loan is repaid (S. 1041).

Analysis. The moving-average loan rate is determined differently in different bills, but the general idea in all of them can be illustrated by the administration's bill (S. 501) for wheat, feed grains, and cotton. Starting with 1986 crops, the loan rate would be 75 percent of the national average price received by farmers for the three immediately preceding crops. If this approach had been used for corn in 1985, for example, the loan rate would have been $(2.68 + 3.25 + 2.65)/3 \times 0.75 = 2.15$, instead of the 1985 loan rate under current law of 2.42. Thus the moving-average loan rate would generate prices well below the current prices that are believed to be hindering exports. In keeping loan rates low, the 75 percent "discount" is more important than the moving average. Current law establishes a similar but more complicated procedure for determining the loan rate for cotton, which is based on the lower of 85 percent of a three-year annual average market price or 90 percent of the price in the first fifteen weeks after July 1 in the current year. The moving-average feature could make loan rates follow markets either more or less closely than under current law. In a period like 1972–1975, the tendency would be for loan rates to rise substantially when they have no appreciable effect (because market prices are as high anyway) but then be stuck at unrealistically high levels for one or two years if markets weaken.

The "market loan" approach, which permits the farmer to repay a CCC loan at the market price, prevents the commodity from accumulating in CCC stocks when markets weaken. It assures the farmer of receiving the loan rate for grain without actually holding the market price at the loan rate. It is essentially the same as eliminating the loan program but guaranteeing the producer's price. Since this guarantee is already available through deficiency payments, the market-loan approach merely extends this approach with a paid guarantee at harvest time equal to the loan rate.

With respect to pros and cons, the discounted moving-average loan rate appears to have wide support because it provides flexibility in loan rates without placing political pressures on the secretary of agriculture as discretion to adjust loan rates does. The main disadvantage is that a particular series of events might make the formula yield less flexibility than needed, as in the scenario outlined above. The generally positive reaction to the discounted moving-average cotton loan rates improves the chances for this approach.

Summary. The market-loan approach is a more radical change, essentially eliminating market price support. Its advantages are as follows:

1. Since the United States would no longer be maintaining a price umbrella for world grain markets, this approach in the short run would permit U.S. grain to be exported (rather than going into CCC stocks) and in the long run would not offer the incentive for expanding production abroad that current loan rates do. The general result would be stronger demand for U.S. grain.
2. Since the CCC would no longer acquire burdensome stocks of grain, storage costs would be saved and the necessity for periodic acreage controls removed.

The disadvantages are these:

1. There might be substantial budgetary costs to make up the CCC's losses when market prices fell below the loan rate.
2. The price stabilization that CCC stocks have sometimes provided in low-production years would not be available.

At the end of July 1985, both Agriculture committees had approved the market-loan approach. Secretary of Agriculture Block, however, expressed opposition on budgetary grounds, implicitly threatening a veto.[4]

Target Prices and Deficiency Payments

Target prices and deficiency payments are shaping up as the most contentious issues in the 1985 farm bill discussions. The administration bill (S.

501) phases out deficiency payments as follows: The target price would be 100 percent of the same three-year average used in calculating the loan rate in 1986, 95 percent in 1987, 90 percent in 1988, 85 percent in 1989, 80 percent in 1990, and 75 percent in 1991 and subsequent years. The payment per bushel would be the target price minus the national year-average market price received by producers. Since the price received is supported at the loan rate, by 1991 deficiency payments would be completely phased out for wheat, feed grains, cotton, and rice—all the commodities now under target price protection. Essentially the price guaranteed would be reduced, beginning in 1987, by 5 percent per year plus the percentage decline in the three-year average price.

The other omnibus bills do not phase out target prices, and several freeze 1986 target prices at 1985 levels, with cuts beginning in 1987 (S. 908). The Boschwitz-Boren bill (S. 1041) replaces target prices by transition payments on 1985-base production, equal to $0.94 per bushel for corn, $1.42 per bushel for wheat, and $0.26 per pound for cotton. These payments are gradually reduced to 50 percent of their initial level in 1986.

The House and Senate committee discussions, particularly a series of votes in the Senate committee in July, have moved completely away from a cut in target prices in 1986. Instead, the question is whether target prices should be frozen for two years or four.

Analysis. To estimate the 1986 target prices under the administration's bill, assume that corn, wheat, and cotton will all have market prices for 1985 and 1986 crops just above their loan rates. This implies three-year averages that determine the 1986 and 1987 target prices as shown in table 2. The 1986 target prices would be substantially reduced from 1985 for wheat and cotton. In 1987 they would again be substantially reduced for all the crops covered. Cuts of this size would be expected to reduce budgetary outlays for target prices by about $5 billion in 1986 and another $8 billion in 1987, except that the concomitant loan rate reductions would increase budget exposure enough to lose about half the budgetary gain.

An analysis carried out at the University of Missouri and Iowa State University suggests that the administration's bill would result in an average farm income loss of $7 billion in 1986–1990.[5] Consumers and taxpayers, however, would gain slightly more than that amount.

The Boschwitz-Boren approach maintains relatively large payments as a cushion when loan rates are cut, and none of the other proposals cuts farmers' incomes as sharply as the administration's bill. Indeed, it seems most likely, at the time of the August recess, that farm income will not be cut at all.

The notion that target prices should be cut derives not only from a desire to reduce budgetary exposure but also from a belief that the target-price guarantees have encouraged farmers to keep on producing large quan-

TABLE 2

TARGET PRICES UNDER ADMINISTRATION BILL, 1982–1987

	Farm Price	Past-Three-Year Average	Target Price
		Wheat (dollars per bushel)	
1982	3.55	—	—
1983	3.53	—	—
1984	3.37	—	—
1985	3.35	3.48	4.38
1986	2.60	3.42	3.42
1987	—	3.11	2.95
		Corn (dollars per bushel)	
1982	2.68	—	—
1983	3.25	—	—
1984	2.65	—	—
1985	2.60	2.86	3.03
1986	2.23	2.83	2.83
1987	—	2.49	2.36
		Cotton (cents per pound)	
1982	59.1	—	—
1983	66.0	—	—
1984	58.4	—	—
1985	58.0	61.2	81.0
1986	—	60.8	60.8

tities of crops in the 1980s despite the lack of a market for them. Cutting the target prices takes away this incentive. The Boschwitz-Boren approach is to limit the supply response to target prices by determining payments on the basis of historical (1985) production rather than current-year production.

Summary. To summarize the pros and cons of cutting target prices, the advantages are (1) budgetary savings, and (2) reduction of the incentive to overproduce and therefore removal of the need for acreage controls. The disadvantage is that farm income would fall.

For the target-price crops, acreage controls are used to control production under current law. They have been in effect every year since 1981 and were particularly important in 1983. In that year the payment-in-kind (PIK) program idled about 80 million acres, the largest acreage reduction program ever. The PIK program and unfavorable summer weather resulted in substantially higher prices for grains and cotton. But as prices came back down in 1984 and 1985 while U.S. export markets weakened and exports of foreign competitors increased, the PIK program, and acreage controls generally, were seen as not being the answer to U.S. farmers' problems. Consequently, most of the 1985 farm bills do not rely on production control measures, although most continue at least temporarily the secretary of agriculture's authority to introduce acreage diversion programs. The "high loan rate" bills—H.R. 2017 (Rose), H.R. 1656 (Glickman), S. 1083 (Harkin)—implicitly involve some kind of supply management, and S. 1051 (Zorinsky) and H.R. 1912 (Stenholm) indicate some sympathy for production controls by giving farmers a chance to vote for them and by rationalizing the allocation of production among producers.

One form of acreage reduction is sufficiently popular that it seems certain to become part of the 1985 act—the idea of holding out of production cropland that is particularly subject to water or wind erosion. As in the case of export promotion, the secretary of agriculture has already announced his intention of establishing such a program under existing authority, apart from its formal incorporation in the omnibus farm bill.

The proposals contain two main elements: (1) a "sodbuster" provision that would deny deficiency payments and other program benefits to farmers who add fragile lands to their cropland (the Boschwitz-Boren bill would also deny them to farmers who have done so in the immediate past); and (2) a paid diversion program in which farmers would sign long-term contracts taking cropland out of production. Either the amount paid per acre would be set by the Agriculture Department, or farmers could offer rental rates that they would accept and the department would choose among their bids. The scale of the program would be 20 to 30 million acres.

Analysis. The main economic issue concerning production controls is how much they can do to increase farm commodity prices and over what period. It is well established for the grains that, in the short run, when production falls, prices rise by a larger percentage than the production decline. That is, demand is inelastic. But over the longer term, especially for exported commodities, higher U.S. prices are expected to have a much greater effect on sales. At some point production controls become counterproductive, actually reducing net returns to producers. Avoidance of production controls as a major policy instrument in a multiyear farm bill is linked to concerns about the market-shrinking consequence of sustained production controls.

Past acreage retirement programs have also been criticized for being ineffective. In 1985, for example, the wheat program is ostensibly idling 30 percent of wheat acreage, as it has in the preceding two years. But yield per acre has risen enough to offset a great deal of the acreage reduction. "Slippage" between expected and actual output reduction arises because farmers place in this program their least productive acreage or acreage that would have lain fallow anyway and because they use more nonland inputs on the acreage that remains in production.

Whether slippage is a significant problem depends in part on the objective of the acreage control program. If the objective is to reduce output with the least cost to the Treasury in payments to producers, slippage is a real problem. If the objective is to provide financial aid to producers, that aim is achieved even if payments do not reduce output. But we also have to consider the distribution of payments among producers. There may be objections to providing the most financial aid to those producers who are cleverest at receiving diversion payments while keeping on producing.

The diversion of specifically erosion-prone land has immediate appeal, but questions can be raised about this approach, too. If marginal land rents for $40 per acre, a 30-million-acre program will cost $1.2 billion per year. That is a lot to pay farmers for not growing crops on land that, according to this policy, they should not have placed in crop production anyway. As a production control measure, it is not clear that this approach has any advantage over general acreage controls, and it has the same disadvantages. It stands or falls, therefore, primarily on its contribution to soil conservation and environmental improvement. Although those ends are politically widely accepted, the evidence is weak on whether a program of this kind will contribute significantly toward achieving them or whether the social gains justify the substantial costs involved.

Moreover, although there is disagreement on just how much fragile cropland there is and how serious the potential erosion problem is, it seems widely agreed that the fragile lands are located in geographically concentrated areas in relatively few states. The political pressure, however, is to have land in all states and practically all congressional districts eligible for long-term paid diversion. This means that the program is likely to diverge from retiring a scientifically chosen allocation of marginal lands. The House bill, for example, was amended to allow any land, erodable or not, to be eligible for long-term diversion payments if salinity threatens its productivity. This provision aids owners of certain irrigated lands, particularly in

California, but contributes nothing to conservation goals.

Summary. Overall, the advantages of production controls are as follows:

1. Since market forces drive up farm prices, budgetary costs are reduced.
2. Since foreigners buy much of the output, they pay for part of our farm program.
3. Controls can be tailored to preserve fragile lands.

The disadvantages are these:

1. U.S. consumers pay higher prices.
2. The export market shrinks.
3. Slippage reduces the cost effectiveness and skews the program's benefit distribution.
4. The idled land, apart from the most marginal acreage, is a wasted resource.

AID TO FINANCIALLY PRESSED FARMERS

As the Ninety-ninth Congress convened in January 1985, the financial situation in agriculture was one of the first items taken up. A bill passed by both houses and sent to President Ronald Reagan would have had lenders write down some farm loans and would have provided greatly expanded federal guarantees for loans to farmers who could not qualify for commercial loans because of their weak financial condition. It was said that without substantial governmental action many farmers would not even be able to obtain loans for planting crops and the whole agricultural economy of some areas would thus be endangered. In February President Reagan vetoed the legislation, apparently on the grounds that emergency credit programs initiated in the fall of 1984 were sufficient, that the financial crisis was not so pervasive or deep as had been implied, and that the legislation would create unacceptable budgetary risks. No attempt was made in Congress to override the veto. This meant that any credit relief program would be attached to omnibus farm legislation.

Analysis. The credit features of the 1985 bills constitute not so much emergency relief measures as revisions of the institutions that provide credit to the financially weakest farmers. The main such institution is the Farmers Home Administration (FmHA), which provides loans to farmers at subsidized interest rates for farm ownership and operating purposes, with special loan programs for disaster relief (in case of crop failure and, in some instances, "economic emergency"). To be eligible for subsidized loans, farmers must be certified—mainly by commercial bankers—as unable to obtain credit elsewhere.

The administration's bill (S. 501/H.R. 1420) would substantially scale back FmHA activity on two fronts: it would no longer provide disaster relief loans for crops in counties where crop insurance is available; and it would remove FmHA from direct operating loans to farmers, substituting FmHA guarantees on commercial loans—reimbursing lenders for 75–90 percent of an uncollectable farm loan.

The other bills for the most part omit credit provisions. S. 616 (Helms) has a more modest reduction in FmHA activities. H.R. 2100 (de la Garza) and S. 1051 (Zorinsky) attempt to make FmHA a more liberal lender.

Summary. Taking the main issue as a general one of whether to provide further credit relief to farmers who need it, the arguments in favor are as follows:

1. Aid to people in trouble is an accepted role of the federal government generally, and some farmers are in deep trouble.
2. Prevention of widespread farm failures would insure against, or at least reduce, "ripple effect" economic losses throughout rural communities.
3. If the financial crunch is not resolved in 1985, it will be even worse in 1986.

The arguments against are these:

1. Most farmers are not on the verge of business failure, and subsidizing those who are is unfair to others, more prudent or lucky in the past, who must make do without aid.
2. A financial bail-out can be only a short-term palliative and will only postpone the inevitable for many farmers.
3. The signal that investments in farm assets that go sour will be bailed out by the government will rekindle the overpricing of farm assets that was the chief creator of the current problem.

Dairy Program

Policy for the milk and dairy products sector is one of several issues not addressed in the discussion of omnibus policy instruments, several of which pertain only to the grains and cotton.

In addition to the main omnibus bills, three bills, H.R. 2616 (Frank), H.R. 2464 (Pashayan), and S. 1069 (Leahy), are specifically addressed to the dairy program. The dairy program is especially contentious because of longstanding budgetary costs, large CCC stocks, and regional conflicts related to milk marketing orders. The bill reported by the House of Representatives subcommittee that handles the dairy program has antagonized many in the industry because it appears to favor producers in the South and West over the traditional upper Midwest dairy region.

Existing law has already cut the milk support price from $13.10 per hundred pounds in 1982 to $11.60 in the summer of 1985. Still, CCC stocks of powdered milk, butter, and cheese remain unacceptably large.

The main options being considered are these:

1. Maintain the current program structure, but cut the support price gradually until overproduction—as measured by CCC "removals" of dairy products—ceases. This approach is taken in S. 616, H.R. 2100, S. 908/ H.R. 1965, and S. 1051.

2. Replace the current program with direct payments, as for grains. Then reduce the market support price immediately, but maintain target price payments. S. 1041 (Boschwitz-Boren) cuts the support price to $10.60, with a transition payment beginning at $1.50 per hundredweight on base production. The administration bill places a milk target price on the same kind of formula it introduces for grains.

3. Institute a production control program in which producers contract to reduce output from a base period. This approach was tried for a fifteen-month period (January 1984–March 1985) and has been included in the bill reported by the House Agriculture Committee. It has pros and cons generally analogous to those for acreage controls for grains, but dairy farmers are assessed a fee of forty cents per hundredweight on the milk they produce to finance a large part of payments to producers for milk not produced. So it is a budget-reducing measure.

Other Commodity Programs

Although they have received little attention in the committee deliberations, programs for some commodities other than grains, cotton, and dairy products have drawn a few reform proposals. Wool, for example, does not involve large budgetary outlays, but payments to producers have been equal to the market value of wool in some recent years. Honey does not require payments, but the support price is so high that the CCC has acquired a large fraction of last year's honey output.

Sugar actually earns money for the U.S. Treasury through import tariffs, but import quotas make the U.S. price (New York basis) of raw sugar 21.5 cents per pound, compared with 4.5 cents per pound on the world market. This difference is estimated to cost consumers about $3 billion per year.

The administration bill cuts the loan rate from 18 cents (achieved not by CCC loans but by quotas maintaining the market price at the New

York–equivalent market support price of 21.5 cents) to the lower of 12 cents or 75 percent of the average price for the past three years. Congressional action is still uncertain, with little pressure for changes from current law.

Peanuts and tobacco do not involve large budget costs but impose costs on consumers through production controls. Policy for these commodities is based on the allocation of marketing quotas to producers. Operational and slippage problems are less than for acreage controls because of the greater ease of supervising marketing channels involving relatively few buyers. The administration bill changes peanuts to the target-price approach and ends production and marketing controls, but no other bills follow this path. The only proposal for tobacco before committee markup was a bill introduced by Representative Rose and Senator Gore (H.R. 2600/S. 1205), which would finance the tobacco price support program with 2 cents of the 16 cents federal excise tax on cigarettes. Currently, assessments on tobacco growers finance price support (stockpiling) activities.

Other Provisions

Three general provisions of current law have received much discussion in past legislative debates, but less in 1985: P.L. 480 (Food for Peace); the farmer-owned Reserve program; and payment limitations.

P.L. 480. This program involves roughly $1 billion per year in heavily subsidized exports and in some cases outright aid to lower-income countries. The program has been perhaps the most stable feature of U.S. farm policy since the mid-1950s. It has been criticized for its cost to U.S. taxpayers, for being too much a tool of surplus disposal and foreign policy aims rather than of humanitarian food aid concerns (for example, tobacco shipments to Egypt), and for hindering agricultural development in recipient countries. Nonetheless, the program has survived intact for thirty years, and no proposals are being considered for serious reform of it, not even in the administration's bill. It is most likely that funding will be increased.

Farmer-owned Reserves (FOR). This program was called the keystone of President Jimmy Carter's program as incorporated in the 1977 act and maintained with many changes in detail to the present. It was originally seen as a stabilization program as much as a price support program—one that would make commodities available in times of shortage. As the 1970s recede in memory, this function no longer draws much interest. Surpluses look permanent (just as they did in 1970).

The administration bill and several others eliminate the FOR. Most bills, however, retain it with modest changes. It does not seem to be an important issue to people on either side.

Payment Limitation. No person under current law can receive more than $50,000 in deficiency payments. This limit affects mainly large cotton and rice producers. The administration bill reduces the maximum to $20,000 in 1986 and $10,000 after 1987. S. 616 (Helms) cuts the limit about as far, as does S. 250 (Pressler), but most of the bills maintain the $50,000 limit. S. 1041 (Boschwitz-Boren) increases it to $63,000 in 1986.

The argument in favor of limiting payments is basically that the largest farms are doing well enough and do not need payments. A counterargument is that for programs requiring acreage diversion to participate in payments, excluding large farms makes it difficult for acreage diversion to work. But mainly it seems to be an issue of self-interest of small as compared with large farms. A survey of Maryland farmers yielded the following responses to the statement "Most benefits should be given to smaller farms."[6]

	Agree	*Disagree* (percent)	*Not Sure*
Operators of			
Small farms	79	14	6
Large farms	19	74	7

It is not yet clear what either house will decide on the payment limitation issue, but committee discussion indicates a reluctance to cut below the $50,000 ceiling.

Notes to Text

1. Bureau of National Affairs, *Economic Developments,* no. 20, January 30, 1985. H.R. 1420 was introduced by Representative Edward R. Madigan (R-Ill.).

2. See David Rapp, "Doubts about Export Programs May Derail Farm Policy Changes," *Congressional Quarterly,* June 8, 1985, pp. 1103–6.

3. *Washington Post,* June 13, 1985.

4. Bureau of National Affairs, *Economic Developments,* no. 148, August 1, 1985; *Des Moines Register,* August 3, 1985.

5. S. R. Johnson, A. Womack, W. Meyers, R. Young, and R. Jolly, "The Administration Proposal for the 1985 Farm Bill," *FAPRI Staff Report,* no. 3-85, University of Missouri and Iowa State University, March 1985.

6. E. H. Brown and J. Charlesworth, "Maryland Farmers' Views on Agricultural and Food Policy," University of Maryland, AREIS Information Service no. 33, May 1985.

Selected AEI Publications

U.S. Agricultural Policy: The 1985 Farm Legislation, Bruce L. Gardner, ed. (1985, 385 pp., cloth $22.95, paper $12.95)

Food and Agricultural Policy for the 1980s, D. Gale Johnson, ed. (1981, 229 pp., cloth $1

Essays in Co *t,* Phillip Cagan, e

American D *fits, and Options,*

The Admin

The AEI Eco)0; single copy, $2

• *Mail ord* TE, 1150 Seventeent *handling, add 10 perc* *prepaid orders)* • *toll free* 800-424-287 *nge without notice.*

The Americ mpetition of ideas thr bjectives: (1) to exter increase research on academic community The areas studied by y, Fiscal Policy, Go ns, Legal Policy, National Defense Studies, Political and Social Processes, and Religion, Philosophy, and Public Policy. For the $49 annual fee, Associates receive

- a subscription to *Memorandum,* the newsletter on all AEI activities
- the AEI publications catalog and all supplements
- a 30 percent discount on all AEI books
- a 40 percent discount for certain seminars on key issues
- subscriptions to any two of the following publications: *Public Opinion,* a bimonthly magazine exploring trends and implications of public opinion on social and public policy questions; *Regulation,* a bimonthly journal examining all aspects of government regulation of society; and *AEI Economist,* a monthly newsletter analyzing current economic issues and evaluating future trends (or for all three publications, send an additional $12).

Call 202/862-6446 or write: American Enterprise Institute
1150 Seventeenth Street, N.W., Suite 301, Washington, D.C. 20036